MY NEIGHBORHOOD

Portia Summers

Enslow Publishing
101 W. 23rd Street
Suite 240
New York, NY 10011
USA

enslow.com

WORDS TO KNOW

apartment—A room or a set of rooms where people live.

community—A group of people who live and work together.

donate—Give to a person or a group to help that person or group do something good.

employee—A person who has a job at a place or a company.

residents—The people who live in a place.

vacant—Empty.

volunteers—People who give their time to do work without being paid money.

CONTENTS

A neighborhood is a community. It is made up of all of the people who live and work there.

What Is a Neighborhood?

A community is a group of people who live and work together. There are many different kinds of communities. A town is a community. Schools are communities. A family living in a house is a community.

Neighborhoods are a kind of community. They are made up of the people who live, work, and play in a small part of a city or a town.

Living and Working in the Neighborhood

There are a lot of different kinds of neighborhoods. In a big city with many people, a single block of apartment buildings might be a neighborhood. Small towns have neighborhoods, too. The neighborhood might be a single street or a whole side of town. The people who live and work in that area help each other with the things that they need.

Growing Up in the Neighborhood

Lots of children live in a neighborhood community. These children might play together or share the same bus stop. Older children may babysit the younger children in a neighborhood. Children help bring neighborhood communities together.

Children grow up in all kinds of neighborhoods. They might live in a house or an apartment or another kind of home.

Neighborhood children of all ages come together to ride the bus to school.

Helpful Neighbors

The people who live in a neighborhood are called residents. Often, the residents of a neighborhood help each other. If one person in the neighborhood gets sick, his neighbors might bring him meals or mow his lawn for him. Another neighbor might babysit for a couple with a new baby. There are lots of ways to help our neighbors!

There are many different kinds of people in the neighborhood. Some are young, and some are old. They all need a little help sometimes.

Neighbors are happy to help each other out.

Everyone Lends a Hand

Some projects are too big for one person or even for a small group. Sometimes everyone has to work together. Once a year some communities have a neighborhood clean-up day. The local hardware store may donate garbage bags and work gloves. Neighbors work in teams. Some teams pick up litter. Some clean trash from vacant lots. Others pull garbage out of streams and ponds. Together they make the neighborhood a better place.

Neighborhood Contests

Cooperation is nice, but sometimes a little friendly competition can be fun, too. Neighborhoods have contests to see who has the prettiest holiday lights or the most beautiful garden. Everybody wins, because these things make the whole neighborhood look nice.

Residents pitch in to keep their neighborhood clean.

Who's in the Neighborhood?

Some people in a neighborhood do not actually live there. They work in the neighborhood every day, but they live somewhere else. They are still important members of the neighborhood.

The mail carrier delivers letters and packages to all the neighbors. The plumber comes to the neighborhood to fix people's sinks, tubs, and pipes. The neighbors cannot do everything by themselves. They need help from people from other places, too.

The mail carrier and the garbage collector are two important helpers in all neighborhoods.

Cleaning Up the Streets

It takes lots of different people to keep the streets of the neighborhood clean. In many neighborhoods the town pays a company to pick up the garbage. The town also sends street sweepers and snowplows to keep neighborhood roads clear.

Good Times With Neighbors

Being in a neighborhood can be a lot of fun. One way that neighbors like to have fun is by having a block party. The streets are closed off so that no cars can drive through. Children run around and play while adults talk and cook on the grill. People bring lots of food like salads, side dishes, drinks, and desserts to share. Often there are games, activities, and music. It is a time for neighbors to relax and get to know each other better.

It is nice for neighbors to get together and have fun.

The Community Center

The community center is a place where people from the neighborhood can meet and spend time together. Children come to take art classes. They might come to play games and sports after school. Grown-ups may come to talk about books that they have read. They talk about life in town.

Two kinds of people work at the community center. Employees are paid money for their work. Volunteers give their time for free. Their pay is knowing they are helping other people in the community.

A community center is a place where neighbors play and learn together.

Life in a Neighborhood

A neighborhood is a place where people feel like they belong. They know that their neighbors will help them when they have a problem. They know that the men and women who work in the neighborhood will help them get what they need. They are a community, and they can count on each other!

Coming Together as a Community

Communities need places where people can spend time together in big groups. That is one reason why libraries, playgrounds, and parks are so important.

ACTIVITY: NEIGHBORHOOD HELPERS

In this book, you have learned that there are all different kinds of neighborhoods. The following activity should help you see how your own neighbors come together to help each other.

1. Think about the neighborhood where you live. What kind of neighborhood is it? Is it part of a city? A small town? A street? Who is part of your neighborhood? Remember, people don't have to live in your neighborhood to be a part of it!

2. Make a table like the one shown on page 23. In the left-hand column, write down some people in your neighborhood. Don't forget to include yourself! You can list family members, neighbors, and people like the mailman or other workers.

3. In the right-hand column, list one way that each person helps out your neighborhood. It could be doing a chore for someone, fixing things, or simply being kind and always saying hello. An example is given for you.

4. Now that your list is done, you can see all of the different helpers in your neighborhood. Can you think of ways that you could do more to help your neighbors?

Who's in My Neighborhood?	How Do They Help?
My next-door neighbor	Watches our house when we're away

LEARN MORE

Books

Antill, Sara. *10 Ways I Can Help My Community.*
New York: PowerKids Press, 2012.

Kreisman, Rachelle. *People Who Help: A Kids' Guide to Community Helpers.* South Egremont, MA:
Red Chair Press, 2015.

Waldron, Melanie. *Mapping Communities.* Chicago:
Raintree, 2013.

Websites

PBS Kids
pbskids.org/rogers/buildANeighborhood.html
Build your own neighborhood!

Rights of the People
rightsofthepeople.com/education/government_for_
kids/k-2/neighborhood/index.php
Learn about the people who help in a neighborho

INDEX

Published in 2017 by Enslow Publishing, LLC.
101 W. 23rd Street, Suite 240, New York, NY 10011

Copyright © 2017 by Enslow Publishing, LLC

All rights reserved.

No part of this book may be reproduced by any means without the written
permission of the publisher.

Library of Congress Cataloging-in-Publication Data

Names: Summers, Portia, author.
Title: My neighborhood / Portia Summers.
Description: New York : Enslow Pub., 2017. | Series: Zoom in on communities |
   Audience: K to Grade 3. | Includes bibliographical references and index.
Identifiers: LCCN 2015047560| ISBN 9780766078062 (library bound) | ISBN
   9780766078000 (pbk.) | ISBN 9780766078017 (6-pack)
Subjects: LCSH: Neighborhoods--Juvenile literature. | Neighbors--Juvenile literature.

Classification: LCC HM761 .S86 2016 | DDC 307.3/362--dc23
LC record available at http://lccn.loc.gov/2015047560

Printed in Malaysia

To Our Readers: We have done our best to make sure all website addresses in this
book were active and appropriate when we went to press. However, the author and the
publisher have no control over and assume no liability for the material available on those
websites or on any websites they may link to. Any comments or suggestions can be sent
by e-mail to customerservice@enslow.com.

Photo Credits: Cover, p. 1 romakoma/Shutterstock.com; graphics throughout Kev
Draws/Shutterstock.com (people circle), antoshkaforever/Shutterstock.com (people
holding hands), 3d_kot/Shutterstock.com (houses); p. 4 Purestock/Alamy Stock Photo;
p. 7 Jupiterimages/Thinkstock; p. 8 Design Pics/Thinkstock; p. 10 Jeff Greenough/Getty
Images; p. 12 Hill Street Studios/Eric Raptosh/Getty Images; p. 14 Justin Sullivan/Getty
Images; p. 15 Rob Crandall/Alamy Stock Photo; p. 17 Hero Images/Getty Images; p. 19
KidStock/Getty Images; p. 21 Justin Horrocks/iStockphoto.com.